Henry Ford
The Car Man

Carin T. Ford

Enslow Publishers, Inc.
40 Industrial Road   PO Box 38
Box 398   Aldershot
Berkeley Heights, NJ 07922 Hants GU12 6BP
USA   UK
http://www.enslow.com

Library of Congress Cataloging-in-Publication Data

Ford, Carin T.
    Henry Ford : the car man / Carin T. Ford.
       p. cm. — (Famous inventors)
    Includes index.
    Summary: A simple biography of the man who revolutionized American industry with his assembly-line production of automobiles.
    ISBN 0-7660-2179-3 (hardcover)
    1. Ford, Henry, 1863–1947—Juvenile literature. 2. Industrialists—United States—Biography—Juvenile literature. 3. Automobile industry and trade—United States—Biography—Juvenile literature. 4. Automobile engineers—United States—Biography—Juvenile literature. [1. Ford, Henry, 1863–1947. 2. Industrialists. 3. Automobile industry and trade—Biography.] I. Title. II. Series.
TL140.F6 F663   2003
338.7'6292'092—dc21
                                               2002010405

To Our Readers:
We have done our best to make sure all Internet Addresses in this book were active and appropriate when we went to press. However, the author and the publisher have no control over and assume no liability for the material available on those Internet sites or on other Web sites they may link to. Any comments or suggestions can be sent by e-mail to comments@enslow.com or to the address on the back cover.

Every effort has been made to locate all copyright holders of material used in this book. If any errors or omissions have occurred, corrections will be made in future editions of this book.

Illustration Credits: © Corel Corporation, pp. 4 (car), 9; From the Collections of Henry Ford Museum & Greenfield Village, pp. 6, 7, 8T, 8B, 12T, 12C, 13, 20, 21, 23, 25, 28; Library of Congress, pp. 1, 2, 3, 4 (portrait), 11, 12B, 15, 17, 19, 24, 27, 30; Recreation of first Ford Motor Company building, Pat McCarthy photo, p. 26.

Cover Illustration: Library of Congress (cars © Corel Corporation)

Table of Contents

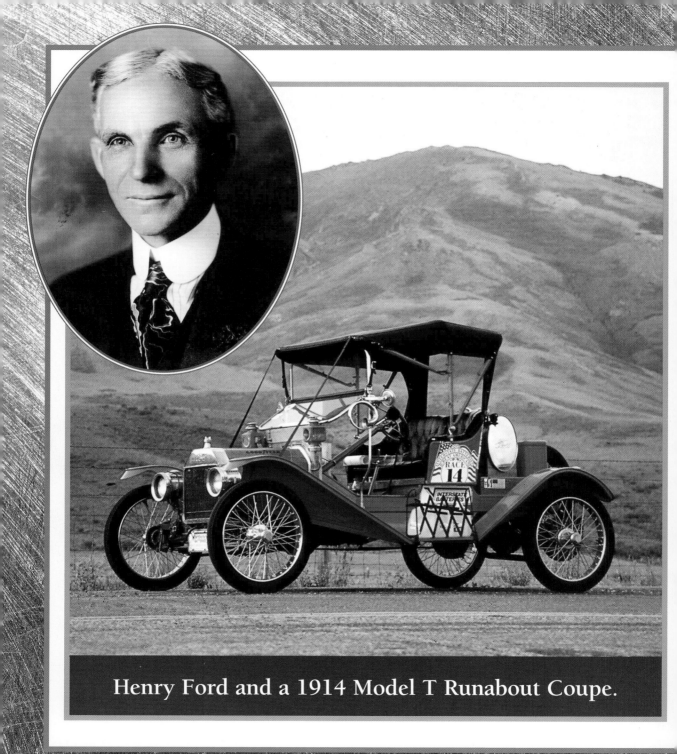

Henry Ford and a 1914 Model T Runabout Coupe.

Chapter 1

A Curious Child

From the time he was a young boy, Henry Ford always had nuts, bolts, and screws stuffed in his pockets. His brothers and sisters hid their wind-up toys from him. They knew if Henry found the toys, he would take them apart. All his life, Henry wanted to know what made things work.

Henry was born on July 30, 1863, near Dearborn, Michigan. His parents were William and Mary Ford.

Over the years, they had five more children—John, Margaret, Jane, William, and Robert.

The Fords lived on a large farm. They grew wheat and vegetables and raised horses, pigs, and cows. William Ford hoped Henry would be a farmer just like him. But Henry was bored by farming. There was only one thing that interested him: machines.

Henry was born in this house.

Henry asked his parents many questions. If they could not give him an answer, Henry would find out for himself.

One day, he was watching a teakettle boil on the stove. The hot steam escaped from the hole in the kettle. Henry began to think. What would happen if the hole were covered up and the steam could not escape?

As a boy, Henry was full of questions.

Henry plugged up the hole—and the kettle exploded. Boiling water sprayed everywhere.

When he was a little older, Henry built an engine next to the fence at his school. It was powered by steam. Like the kettle, it also blew up. Henry and four other boys were hurt, and the fence caught on fire.

In school, Henry did not pay attention. He often got into trouble. Henry was good at reading and

Henry's parents, Mary and William Ford.

arithmetic, but he never learned to spell or write clearly. All his life, writing even a simple sentence was hard for him.

One day, Henry took apart a broken watch. He looked at all the little wheels and springs inside. When he put it back together, the watch worked. Soon he was fixing clocks and watches for all his neighbors.

When Henry was twelve, his mother died. Henry had always been quiet. Now he was so sad that he rarely talked. He spent all his spare time at his workbench.

A few months later, Henry was riding with his father in their farm wagon. To get from place to place in those days, most people rode in a horse and cart. Suddenly, Henry saw a steam engine coming down the road. The engine was moving along on its own. There were no horses pulling it!

Henry jumped off his father's wagon and raced over to the engine. He had many questions for the driver. For years, Henry would think about that amazing machine that moved without horses.

In a steam engine, boiling water creates hot steam. If the steam could not escape, the engine would burst like Henry's teakettle. Instead, the power from the steam is used to make the engine work.

Chapter 2

Work and Marriage

**H**enry had never liked farm life. When he turned sixteen, he moved to the city of Detroit. There, he got a job in a machine shop, working on steam engines.

Henry also worked in a jewelry store, fixing clocks and watches. He had to sit in the back of the store. Customers would not like to see a teenager handling their costly watches.

Next, Henry worked as a machinist for a company

that made engines for steamships. Then, when he was nineteen, he moved back to his father's farm.

William Ford had given Henry some land. Henry cut down trees and ran a sawmill to cut the logs into lumber. He also built a workshop for himself. He spent his spare time working on engines.

Henry also began working part-time for the Westinghouse Company as a steam engine expert.

For a while, Henry cut wood at a sawmill.

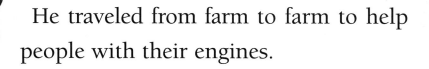

He traveled from farm to farm to help people with their engines.

Two nights a week, Henry took classes at a college in Detroit. He learned skills he would need in business: how to type and how to keep track of money in a business.

Henry took dancing lessons, too. When he was twenty-one, he met Clara Bryant at a dance. She liked hearing Henry talk about watches and engines. She was sure he could do anything he set his mind to.

Henry and Clara were married in 1888. They lived on the farm. Henry used lumber from his own trees to build a small house. During this time, he also built two steam engines. But they did

Henry and Clara liked to dance.

not work very well. Henry thought a gasoline engine would be smaller and easier to use. First, he needed to earn money to pay for tools and materials.

Henry and Clara decided to move to Detroit. There, Henry got a job with the Edison Company. It supplied electric power to people in Detroit.

In 1893, Henry and Clara had a baby boy. They named him Edsel. After a while, Henry became the top engineer at the Edison Company. But this was not what he really wanted to do. More than anything else, Henry wanted to build a machine that could move down the road by itself—an automobile.

This is Henry's first gasoline engine, built in 1893. It uses electricity to create sparks. The sparks make the gasoline burn, and this powers the engine.

Chapter 3

Building an Automobile

The neighbors called him "Crazy Henry," but Henry did not care. He was busy in his woodshed, working on a special kind of car. Sometimes he brought the car engine into the kitchen and asked Clara to help him test it. The room would fill with black smoke, but Clara never complained. Often at night, she threw a shawl over her shoulders and watched Henry work. She was sure he would succeed.

Success at last! Henry rolls out his first car, the Quadricycle.

Other inventors in Europe and the United States had built cars using gas-powered engines. These handmade cars were very expensive, and only rich people could afford them.

Henry wanted to build a car that anyone could buy. He was sure that one day, cars would take the place of the horse and buggy—and trains, too.

Finally, on a rainy spring night in 1896, Henry's

car was ready. Henry had not slept for two nights, but he was not tired. He was too excited.

As Henry moved his car toward the doorway of the shed, he discovered a big problem: It did not fit through the doors. So Henry grabbed a hammer and smashed a large hole in the brick wall! Then he drove his car out onto the dark, wet streets.

Henry called his invention a Quadricycle. He nicknamed it "the baby carriage," saying it looked like one. The car was small and light. It moved on wire wheels like bicycle wheels. Henry steered with a stick attached to the wheels. The car could only go forward; it had no brakes. But it worked.

The next day, Henry took Clara and little Edsel for a drive. After that, Henry drove the car all around Detroit. People gathered in the streets to watch his strange machine cough and bump down the road.

Henry said the Quadricycle looked like a baby carriage.

Chapter 4

Sudden Fame

By 1899, Henry had to choose between his job at the Edison Company and his hobby of making cars. For Henry, the answer was easy. He started a company to make and sell cars.

Henry's company was a failure. At the start of the 1900s, few Americans had ever seen a car. Even fewer owned one. But car races were very popular. In 1901, Henry decided to build a race car. He hoped that if his car did well in the race, he might be able to raise the money to start another car company.

Henry entered his first race when he was thirty-eight years old. Eight thousand people watched as Henry crossed the finish line first.

After that, Henry built an even faster race car. He called it the "999." In a car race, the 999 set an

Henry stands next to the 999 and its driver.

American record. It traveled five miles in a little more than five minutes.

This race made Henry famous.

In 1903, Henry started the Ford Motor Company. It would become the world's biggest car maker.

Henry made eight different kinds of cars in the first five years. He named each car after a letter of the alphabet. He began with Models A and B, and then Models C, F, K, N, R, and S.

Henry was always looking to make his cars even better. He never gave up on his dream of building a good, strong car that everyone could afford to buy.

He finally came up with his ideal car when he created the Model T.

Out for a spin: Clara, above right, and her friend take a drive.

Henry and his son, Edsel, in the Model F.

Chapter 5

The Model T

Henry's Model T Ford went on sale in 1908. At first, it cost $825. That was a lot of money in those days. Henry wanted to find a way to lower the cost of making the cars. Then he could lower the price, too.

Like other cars made at that time, the Model T's were built one by one. Two to three cars were made each day.

Henry set up a moving assembly line in his factory.

Pieces of the car traveled along a moving belt. As the car parts rolled by, each worker stood in one place doing the same job over and over. One worker might fasten a bolt or tighten a nut, but he did not do both of these jobs.

The assembly line saved time and money. A new car could be built in just three hours. Now Henry

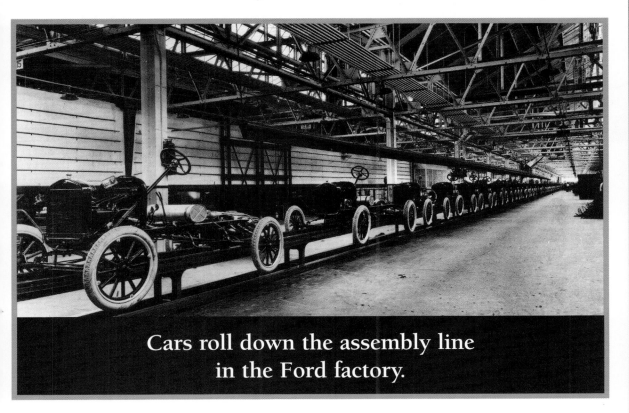

Cars roll down the assembly line in the Ford factory.

could lower the price. By 1913, the Model T was selling for $550. Henry had finally created a car that anyone could buy.

The 1908 Model T was the first car that lots of people could afford to buy.

On the assembly line, each worker did the same task over and over again, all day long. Why would anyone want such a boring job? To get workers, Henry paid them $5 a day. That was twice as much as other factories paid.

By the time Henry was in his middle fifties, half of all the cars in America were Model T's. Nicknamed the "Tin Lizzie," the Model T would sell 15 million cars by 1927.

Henry became one of the richest men in the world. He was also one of the most famous. He became friends with other important men, such as Thomas Edison, who developed the electric light bulb, and Harvey Firestone, who made rubber tires.

Although he was powerful in business, Henry's views on other subjects were not always popular. Henry often spoke out about government and world affairs. He had strong opinions, and many people did

Henry with his friends Thomas Edison, center, and Harvey Firestone, right.

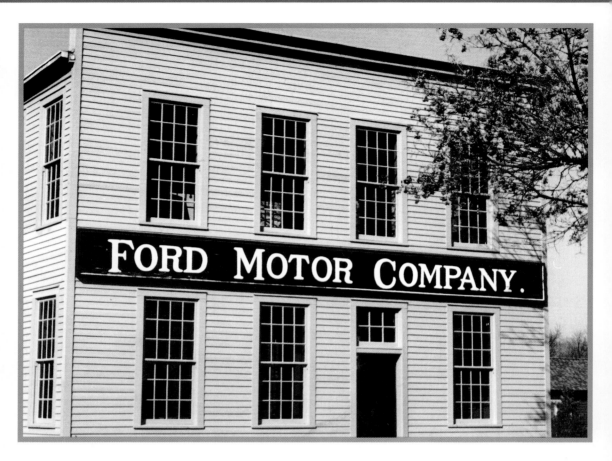

not like what he said. Some people laughed at his ideas, and others were angry.

In 1920, just before Henry turned fifty-seven, he opened the largest car factory in the world. This factory in Dearborn, Michigan, had more than 42,000 workers and ninety different buildings. The Ford

Motor Company also had factories in thirty-three other countries around the world.

Unlike other car companies, Henry made his own parts for the cars. He owned iron mines and steel mills. He brought the materials to his factory on his own railroad and ship lines.

Henry also spent much of his time and money on charities. He set up the Ford Foundation to provide money for education and research projects. He created a historical museum in Greenfield Village, Michigan, to show early American life and the progress of industry.

Henry Ford died in 1947. He was eighty-three years old. He had created a car that many people could afford to buy. With this, he changed the way Americans travel.

Henry Ford filled America's roads with cars.

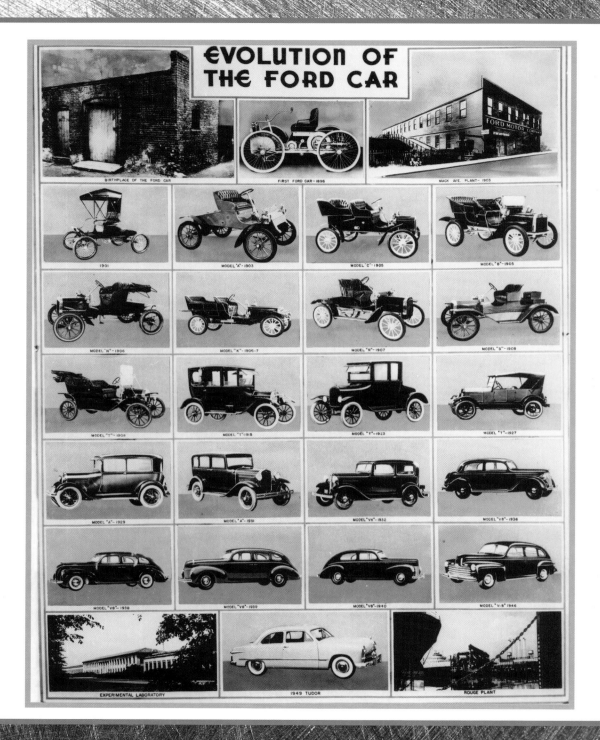

EVOLUTION OF THE FORD CAR

BIRTHPLACE OF THE FORD CAR

FIRST FORD CAR—1896

MACK AVE. PLANT—1903

1901

MODEL "A"—1903

MODEL "C"—1905

MODEL "B"—1905

MODEL "N"—1906

MODEL "K"—1906-7

MODEL "R"—1907

MODEL "S"—1908

MODEL "T"—1908

MODEL "T"—1915

MODEL "T"—1923

MODEL "T"—1927

MODEL "A"—1929

MODEL "A"—1931

MODEL "V8"—1932

MODEL "V8"—1936

MODEL "V8"—1938

MODEL "V8"—1939

MODEL "V8"—1940

MODEL "V-8"—1946

EXPERIMENTAL LABORATORY

1949 TUDOR

ROUGE PLANT

28

Timeline

1863~Born in Dearborn, Michigan.

1879~Moves to Detroit and learns to be a machinist.

1888~Marries Clara Bryant.

1891~Becomes an engineer with Detroit Edison Company.

1896~Builds his first car, the Quadricycle.

1903~Forms the Ford Motor Company.

1908~Introduces the Model T.

1913~Uses moving assembly line to make cars.

1927~Opens the world's largest factory, in Dearborn.

1947~Dies in Dearborn at age 83.

assemble—To fit together the parts of something.

assembly line—A method of building something. The product moves along, and each worker does one job over and over.

Using an assembly line is faster than building one car at a time.

factory—A building where products are made.

industry—A business that manufactures, or makes, a certain product.

machinist—A worker who puts together or repairs machines.

Learn More

Books

Gourley, Catherine. *Wheels of Time: A Biography of Henry Ford.* Brookfield, Conn.: Millbrook, 1997.

Middleton, Haydn. *Henry Ford: The People's Carmaker.* United Kingdom: Oxford University Press, 1997.

Sutton, Richard. *The Car.* Dorling Kindersley, 2000.

Internet Addresses

The Life of Henry Ford
   <http://www.hfmgv.org/exhibits/hf/>

The Museum of Automobile History
   <http://www.themuseumofautomobilehistory.com/>

People and Discoveries: Henry Ford, 1863–1947
   <http://www.pbs.org/wgbh/aso/databank/entries/
   btford.html>

Index